COLORING BOOK

BELONGS TO:

FEAR ME
I'm CUTE

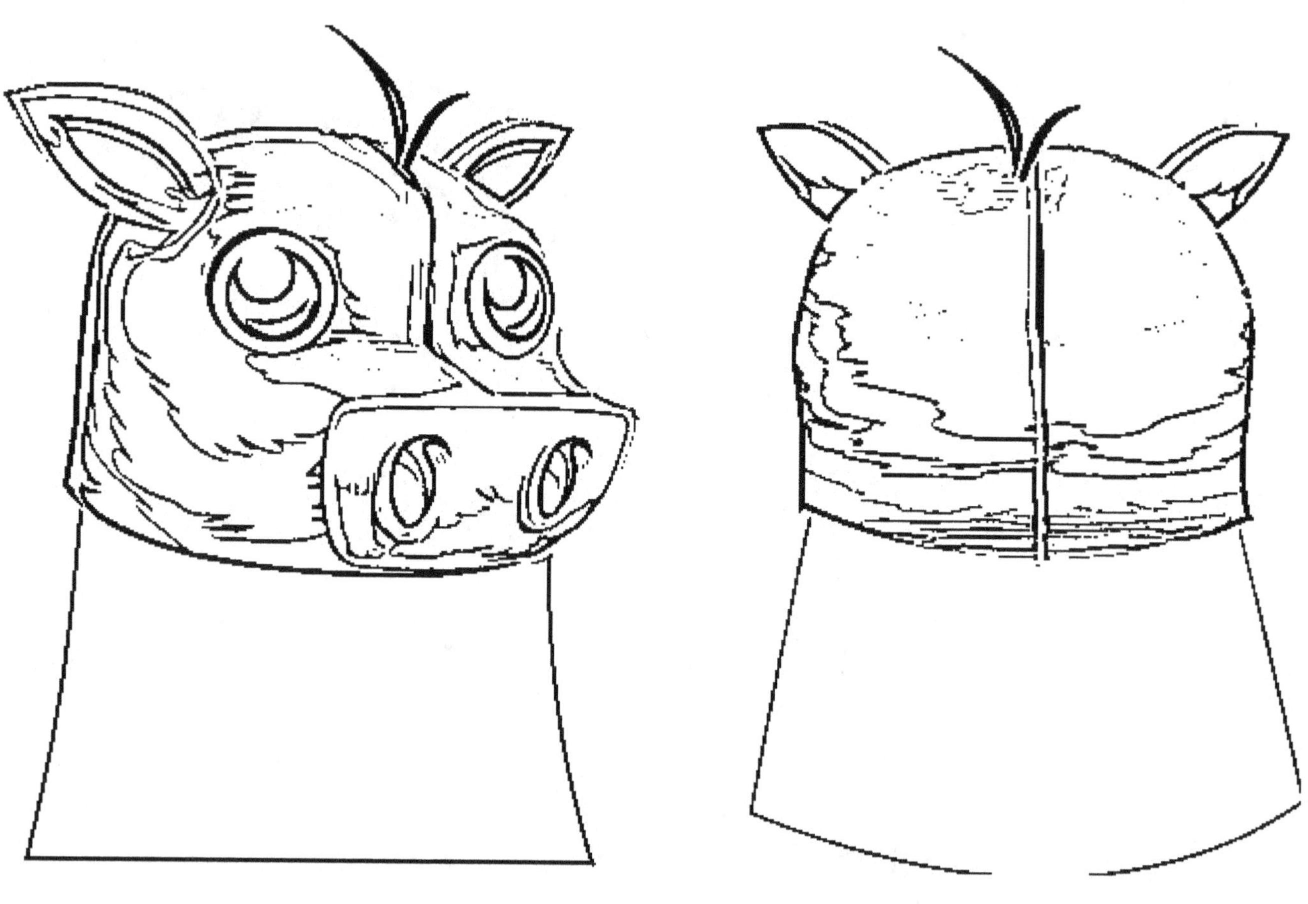

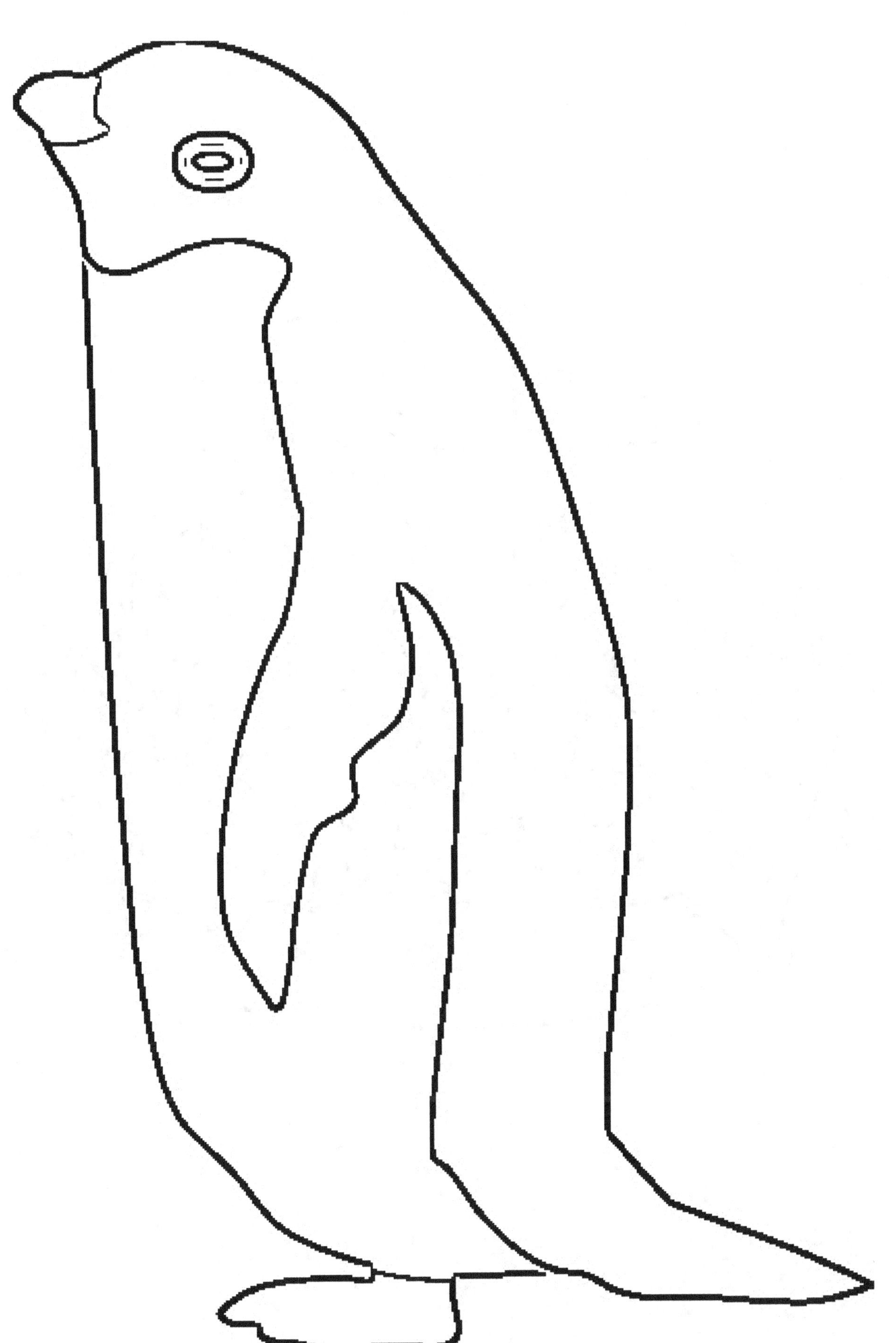

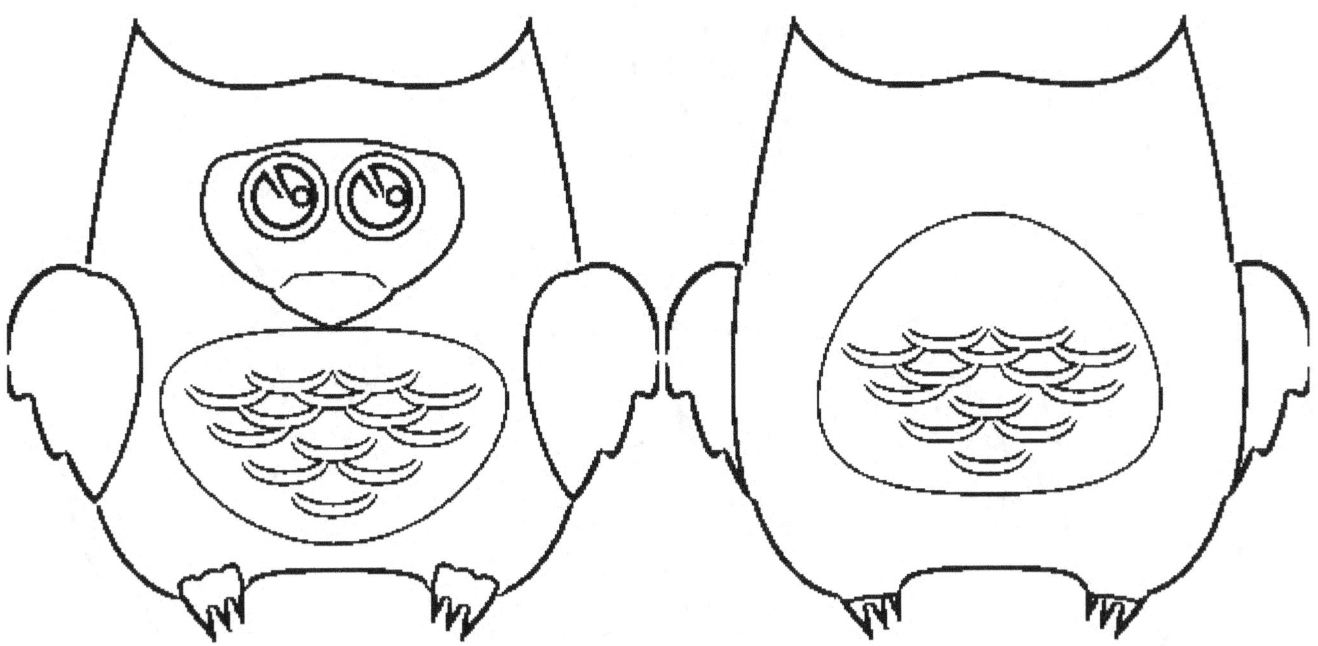

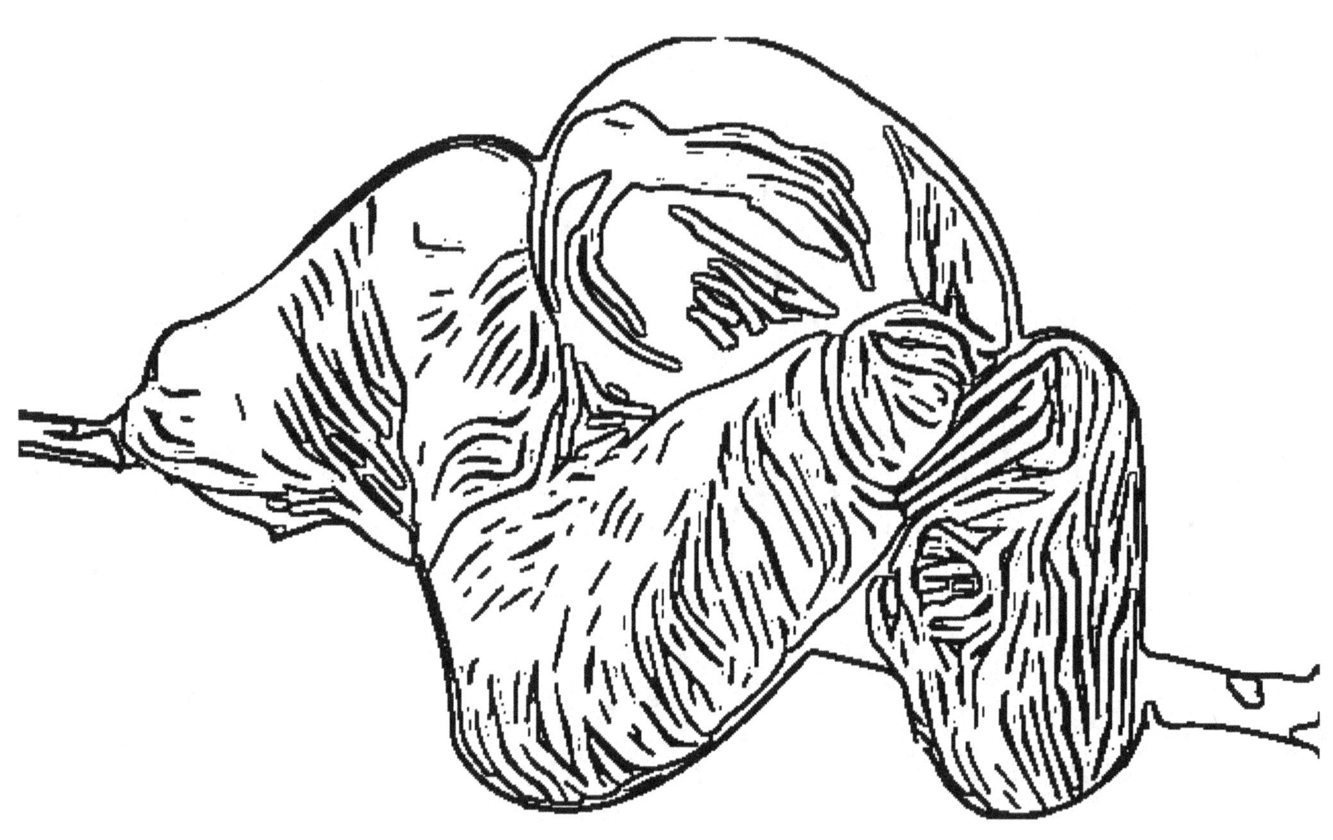

Hello

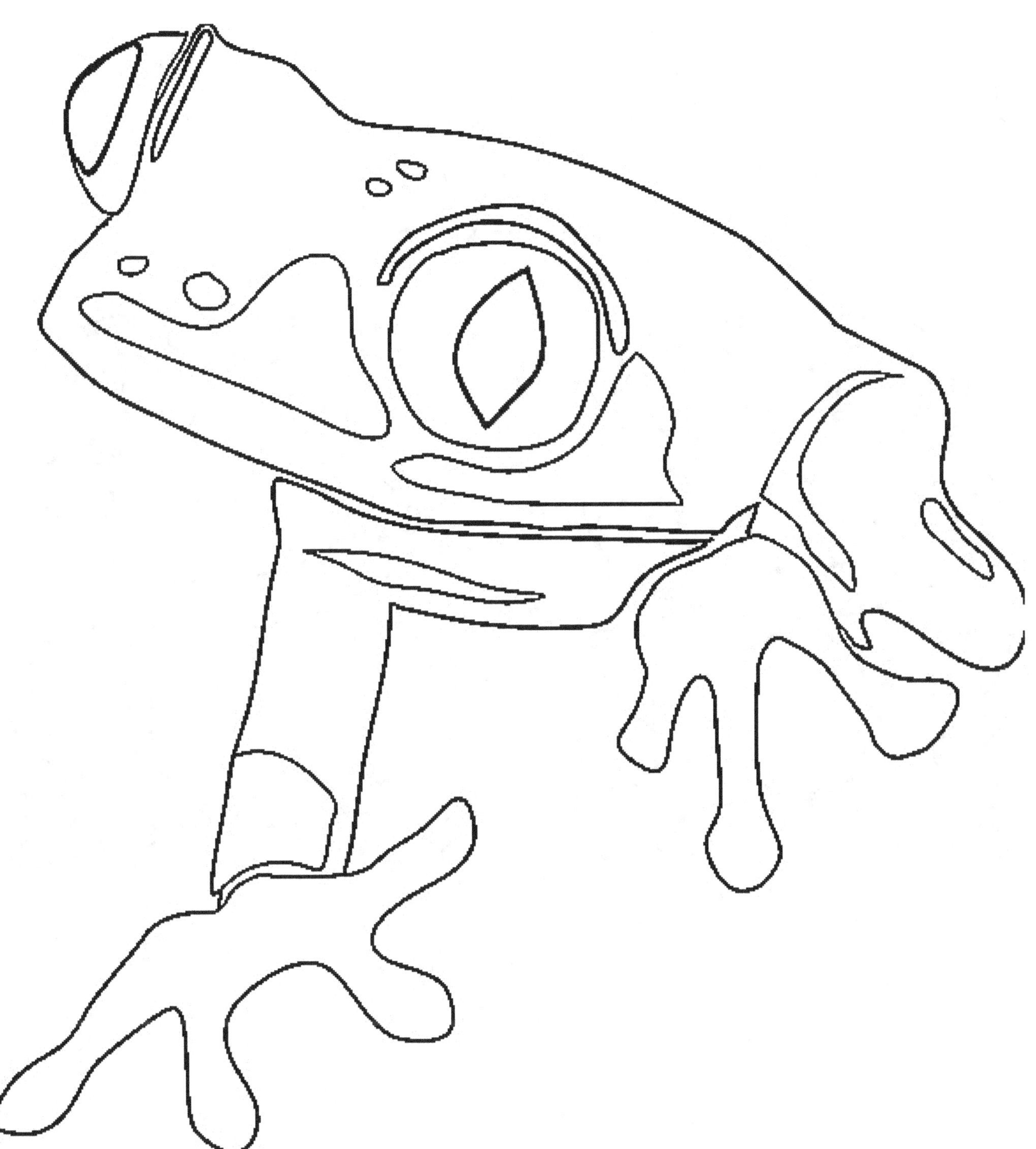

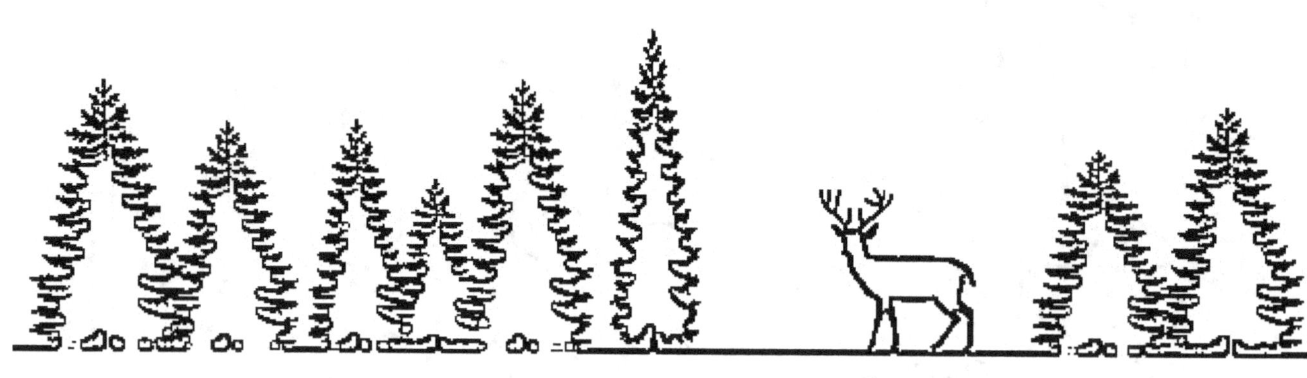

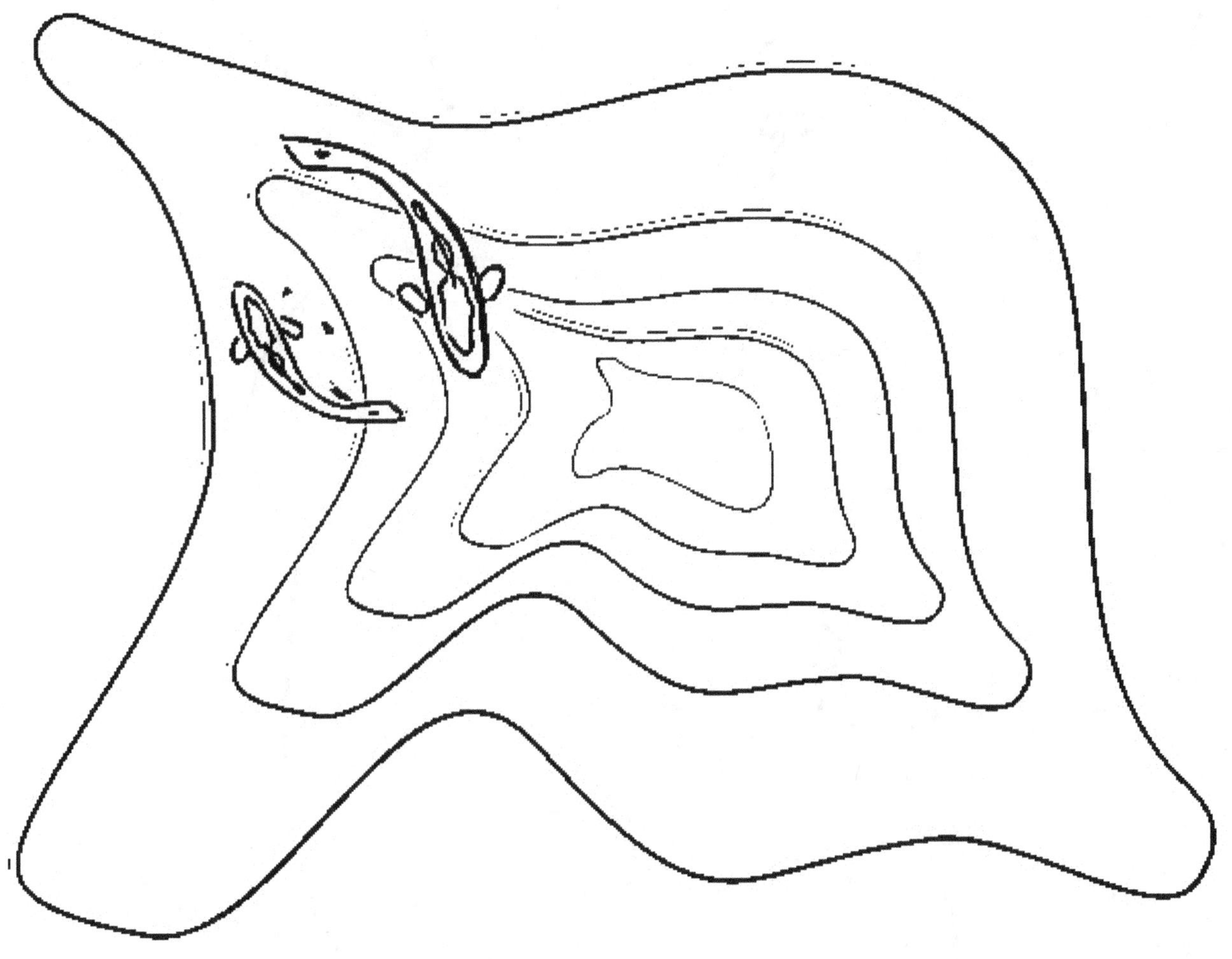

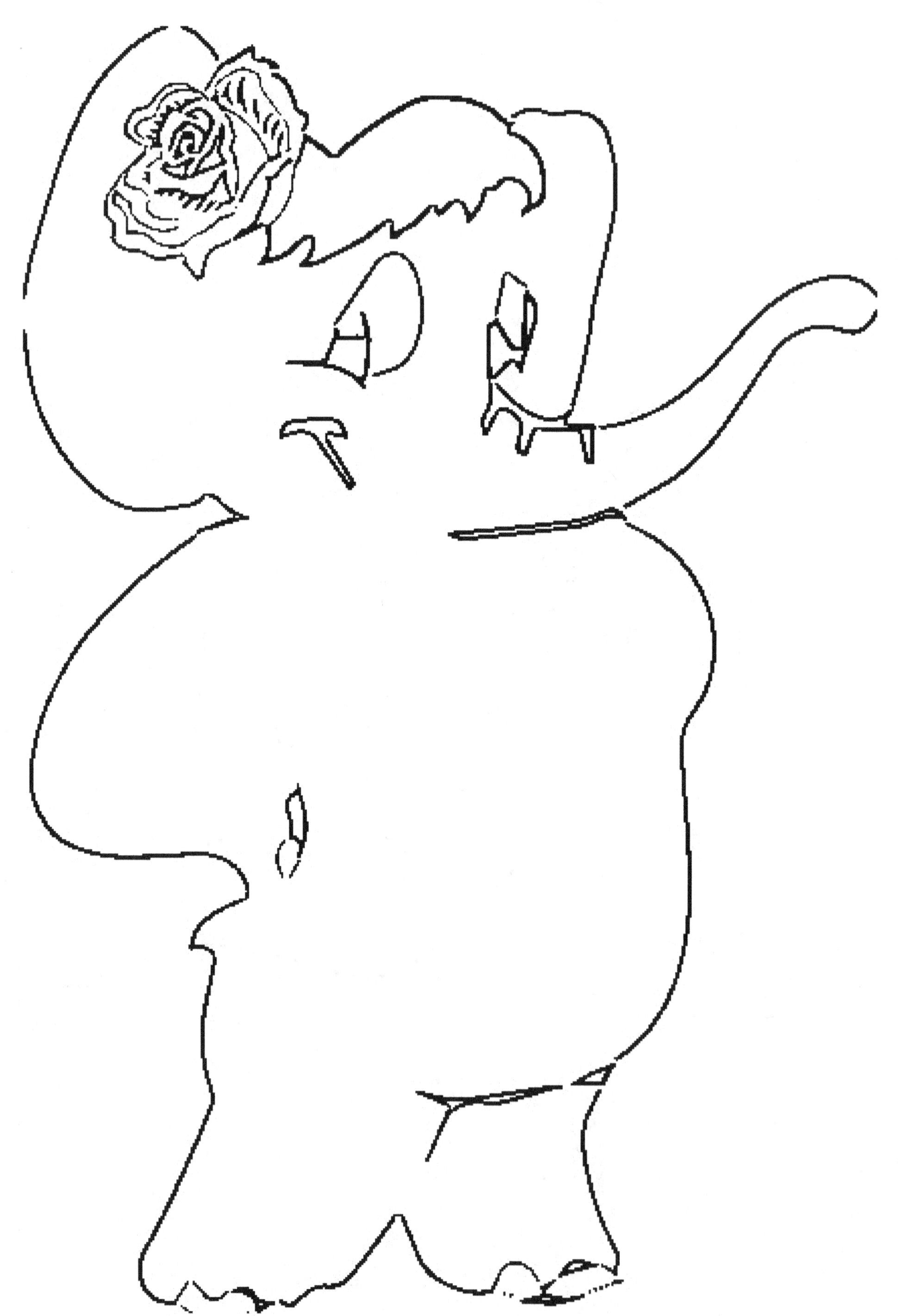

HAPPY EASTER

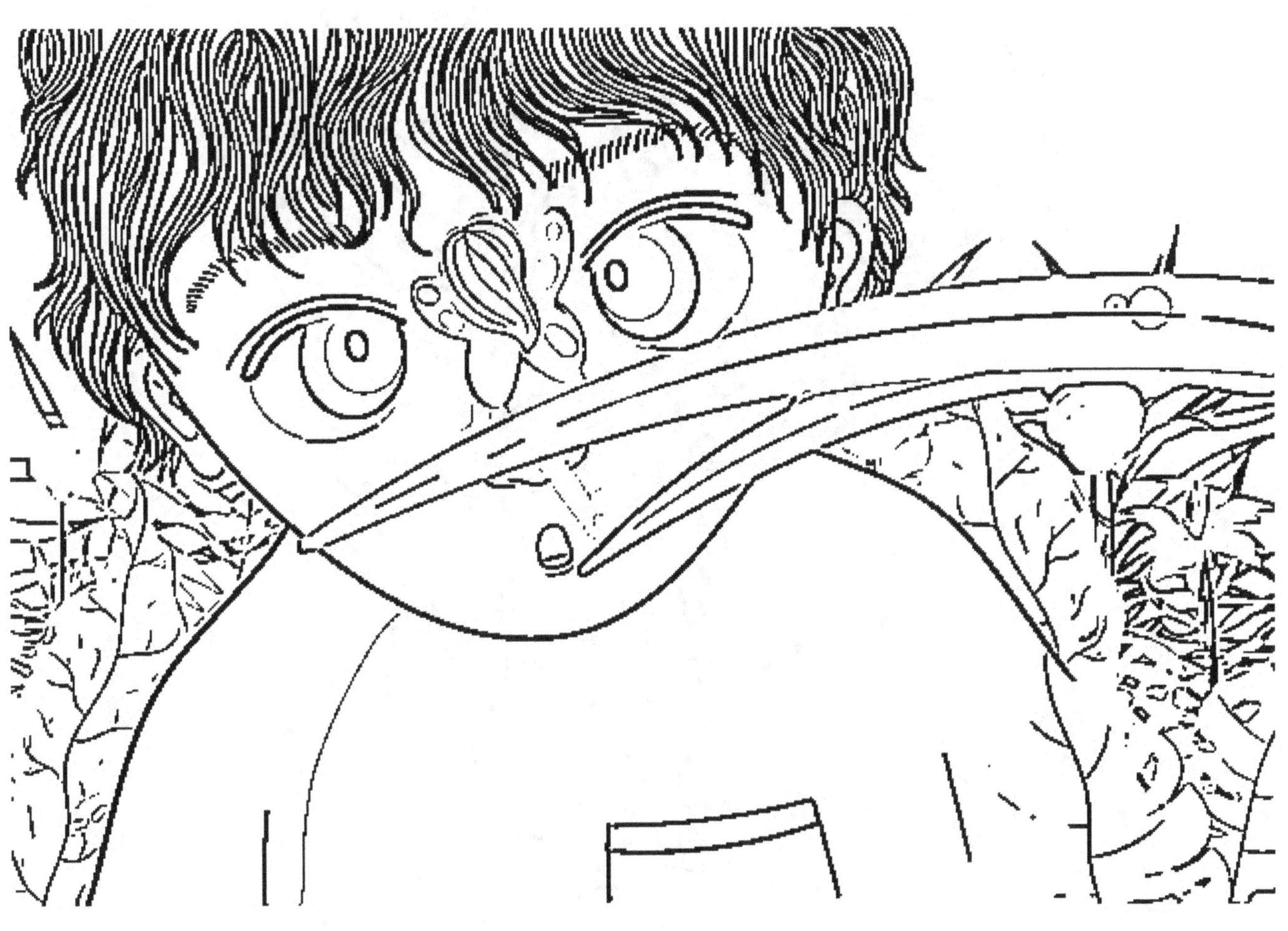

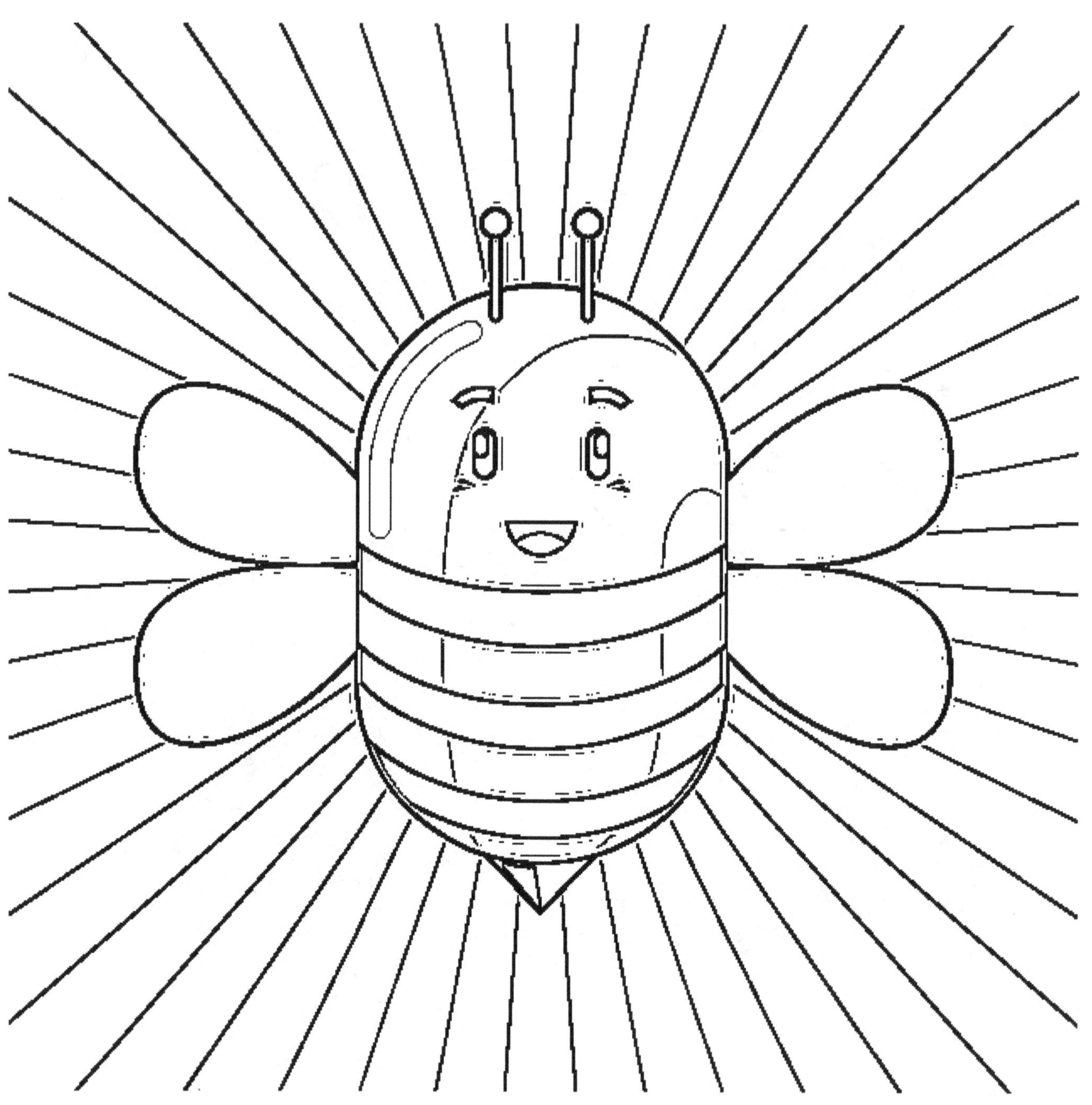